PENCIL, PEN and BRUSH

drawing for beginners
by Harvey Weiss

YOUNG SCOTT BOOKS

REMBRANDT VAN RIJN

GO/WZ   3/75   09311

TABLE OF CONTENTS

Thanks and acknowledgment are due the following museums, institutions, and individuals for their co-operation and help in the preparation of this book: The Metropolitan Museum of Art, New York; The Museum of Modern Art, New York; The Pierpont Morgan Library, New York; The Fogg Art Museum, Harvard University, Cambridge, Massachusetts; The Brooklyn Museum, Brooklyn, New York; The Royal Collection, Windsor Castle, England; Kraushaar Galleries, New York; Standard Oil Company (New Jersey); The French Embassy Press and Information Service, New York; The New York Zoological Society; May, Carla, Bill, John, Miriam. Special thanks are due Maurice Sendak and Joe Lasker, who very generously put their drawings and sketchbooks at the author's disposal.

Illustrations not otherwise credited are by the author.

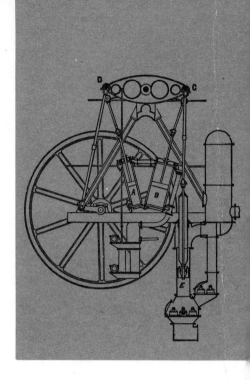

JOE LASKER

Introduction

Drawing is a language without words. Often, this language can tell you things faster and better than words. It is easier to *draw* a smile than to tell about it. A tree can be described more vividly in a drawing than by a series of words. And a diagram will explain—more clearly than any text—how a steam engine works.

In many professions today drawing is an important means of explaining and clarifying ideas. The architect and the dress designer make drawings to show others what they have in mind and to demonstrate what has to be done. The sculptor makes drawings to explore and experiment with his ideas before proceeding to clay or stone. The potter, the airplane designer, the engineer, and, in fact, almost everybody concerned with building and creating uses drawing to explain and clarify ideas.

But drawing can be a very satisfying experience for its own sake. It doesn't have to have a purpose. It doesn't have to be serious or important. Drawing can be great fun whether you keep your picture and frame it, or just crumple it up and throw it away.

LEONARDO DA VINCI

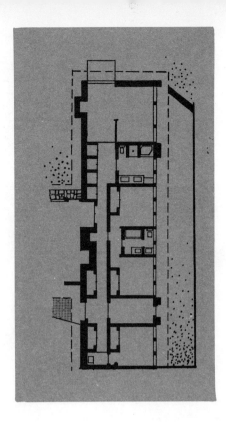

If you drew often enough, you would eventually discover—through trial and error—most of the techniques explained in this book. *Pencil, Pen, and Brush* will speed up the learning process by allowing you to bypass some of the errors you might make if you drew without any help at all.

Each section of this book contains one or more "models." The models are photographs of people and animals and scenes. They are included so that you will have something from which to work. If you work from these photographs and follow the step-by-step directions and illustrations, you will be able to see exactly how a drawing develops. You will learn how to begin, what to try for, what to expect. After you've made one or two drawings from the photograph, you can go off on your own.

The book is divided into six sections. Each section concentrates on one or two particular aspects of drawing. Start at the beginning—and by the time you've worked through the book, you will have an understanding and some experience with the basic elements of drawing.

SAUL STEINBERG

JOE LASKER

MAURICE SENDAK

MAURICE SENDAK

Drawing Animals

What comes to mind when someone says *porcupine?* You probably think of prickly needles. Prickly needles sticking out in all directions—the special quality of porcupines.

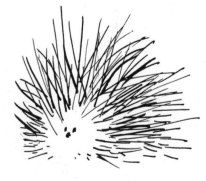

Everything has a special quality, one which distinguishes its appearance or its actions. If you can learn to look for and recognize the special quality of the thing you are drawing, you will have gone a long way toward making a really successful picture.

The artists who drew the animals on the opposite page each captured the special quality of his subject. In the drawing of the bear it is the rough, fuzzy coat. In the chicken it is the fat, bulky look and all the wiggly feathers. Can you tell what special thing the artist found most interesting in his drawing of the lion?

How to Draw an Animal

Most live animals won't oblige by standing still while you draw them, so work at first from the photographs on the page opposite. The elephant's pose is an easy one to draw. Let's start with him.

MATERIALS: Get a pencil that will make a good dark line. You'll also need some sort of pencil sharpener. It's hard to draw with a short, blunted point. Almost any kind of paper will do, but make sure it is a good size—no smaller than 9 by 12 inches. Find a sturdy and well-lighted table on which to work.

1. Before you start to draw, look carefully at the elephant. What is special about him? What makes him look different from a horse or a house or a giraffe? The special quality here is created by the large, heavy forms of the elephant's body—the simple, massive shape.

2. Think of the elephant as a collection of parts; this will help you to get everything in the correct proportion. The body is a big oval (an egg shape), the legs are like tree trunks, the head and ears smaller ovals. Draw in these shapes, keeping them very light. This preliminary drawing is a "map" that shows you where everything is eventually going to be.

3. Now you can start putting in your heavier, final lines. A pencil can make a great variety of lines—quick and sketchy, jiggly, heavy, any kind of line you like. Use a type of line that suits the elephant best.

4. When you have drawn the main shapes, tackle some of the smaller parts, such as the tail and tusks and trunk. Pick out only the most important details. Too many details will confuse the picture.

5. One distinctive feature of elephants is their skin. It has a rough texture—it is a tangle of wrinkles. "Texture" means the kind of surface that an object has. For example, silk has a smooth texture, sandpaper is rough, a wool rug is fuzzy. You can't make the paper itself smooth or rough or fuzzy. But you can *suggest* these qualities by the kind of pencil lines you make. See if you can get the texture of the elephant's skin in your drawing.

6. Finally, when the elephant is finished, you may want to add some background— perhaps a few trees to suggest jungle. How about some grass in the foreground?

After you have completed this drawing of the elephant, try another one. See if you can find a better way of drawing him. You may want to work larger, or smaller. Or you may want to change the pose—perhaps tilt the head, or shift the feet. There is no reason whatever for sticking exactly to the photograph.

When you have drawn the elephant several times, try the lion. Work in the same way as when you were drawing the elephant. Look at the animal carefully. What impresses you as the lion's special quality? Is it his wild, fierce look? Is it his mane? The lion's mane is great fun to draw. Will you use little jagged lines, pretty curls, scratches, blots, scrawls, small circles? Whatever you decide to do, do it *consistently* and the mane will have a definite texture.

There is no one correct way to make a drawing. There are certain steps and methods of working—discussed in this book—that will help you to do what you want. But they are only techniques. It is your privilege and freedom to choose the sort of drawing you want to make. By all means draw a six-legged elephant with polka dots and feathers if the idea intrigues you.

The illustrations on these two pages show how different artists chose to draw a lion. The three drawings on the page opposite are based on the photograph of the lion reproduced on page 8. As you can see, each artist saw the lion very much in his own way!

JOE LASKER

MAURICE SENDAK

H. WEISS

13

MAURICE SENDAK

JACOPO DA PONTORMO

H. WEISS

14

Drawing the Figure

A thoughtful artist once said, "It's not enough to draw what a thing looks like. You have to draw what it *is* and what it is *doing*." This is particularly true when you draw the human figure.

One way to get the feeling, movement, and mood of a figure is to look for and recognize the *action lines*. Action lines reveal the position of the body and show what it is doing. Action lines don't usually appear as such. They are *imaginary* lines. Sometimes just one or two lines can show the action, as in the figures below. Sometimes three or four action lines are needed, as in the juggler.

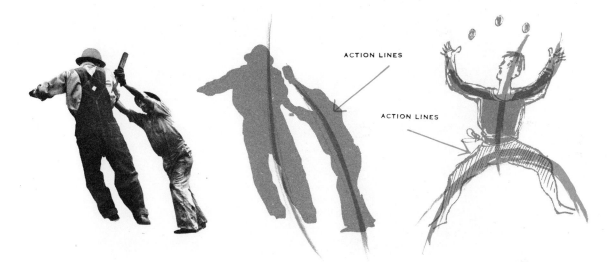

ACTION LINES

ACTION LINES

The fact that these are called "action" lines does not mean that they exist only in moving things. They exist in everything that has a shape or form. Sometimes it is hard to puzzle out what they are—especially if your subject is wearing a lot of bulky clothes, or is all hunched up. But the action lines are always there. Look at some of the drawings on the page opposite. See if you can discover the action lines.

How to Draw the Figure

Of all the busy people on the page opposite, the tennis player has the simplest action lines. So let's start with him.

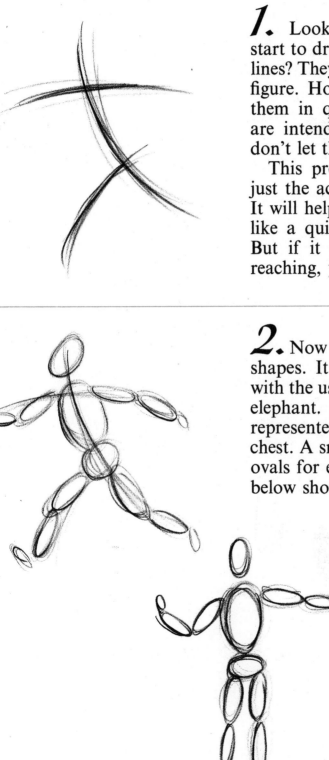

1. Look at the photograph before you start to draw. Can you recognize the action lines? They are quite easy to pick out in this figure. Holding your pencil lightly, sketch them in quickly and roughly. These lines are intended to serve merely as a guide; don't let them get too dark and heavy.

This preliminary drawing, which shows just the action lines, is a sort of warm-up. It will help you to get started. It may look like a quick scribble or a tangle of lines. But if it has the feeling of running and reaching, you are off to a good beginning.

2. Now start to work on your main shapes. It is easiest to draw these shapes with the use of ovals—the way you drew the elephant. Each part of the body can be represented by an oval. A large oval for the chest. A smaller one for the hips. Two long ovals for each leg, and so on. The drawing below shows how this works.

3. Action lines and ovals—when you have this much on paper, you have done the most important part of your drawing. Now you can begin to add your outlines. If the lines you put down at first are not exactly what you want, don't erase them. Ignore them and draw in other lines. Too much erasing would give your drawing a fussed-over, sloppy look. Look at all the lines in the drawings on the page opposite.

4. Skip from one part of the figure to another as your drawing progresses. This is the way to make all the different parts fit in with one another. With your action lines and ovals as a guide, you can be sure of getting everything in the right place. A common fault is to start at the top and work down. Often by the time you reach the feet, the top of the drawing looks like something started by someone else.

5. Once your outline is complete, you can give a little attention to detail. You may want to show some of the wrinkles in the shirt or pants. You may want to put in the socks and belt. But don't include all the little details just because you see them. Include only what you think will look well.

6. The next step is a criticizing one. Put down your pencil. Look at what you have done. Do you see anything you can improve—a line that needs strengthening, a curve that needs changing? Don't struggle too hard with your first drawing, however; start another and see if you can do better.

After you've made two or three sketches of the tennis player, you will probably want to draw something else. Try the wrestlers, or the women fencing. Either subject is exciting—filled with action and many interesting lines and shapes. There are two figures in each case, and the action lines are not quite as simple as the tennis player's. But if you work according to the method that you used for the tennis player—first action lines and then ovals—you won't have any trouble.

Some of the drawings in this book—for example, the one to the right—seem quite small because they have been reduced in size so that they fit on the page. In most cases, the original drawing is a good deal larger than the reproduction.

HONORÉ DAUMIER

Drawing from Life

To draw the figure well, you need much practice. You can learn a good deal by sketching from photographs, but it is hard to find clear and interesting ones. A real-life subject can be seen more clearly, and gives you a more vivid idea of feeling and pose.

Try to get friends or relatives to pose for you in different positions. Get into the habit of sketching the people around you, even if they don't hold still. You can make sketches at the beach, at ball games, looking out the window—wherever there are people.

JOE LASKER

MAURICE SENDAK

JOE LASKER

TINTORETTO

Pen and Ink

The drawings on the facing page were made with pen and ink. This way of working gives you very crisp, sharp lines and dense blacks (and you can't erase). Try some pen-and-ink drawings. Use an old-fashioned penholder and a medium-sized point. If possible, use the special artists' black ink called India ink and a smooth white bond paper (rough, absorbent paper might blot).

Although your final drawing will be in ink, make your action lines and ovals in pencil first. If they are too conspicuous in your finished ink drawing, you can erase them.

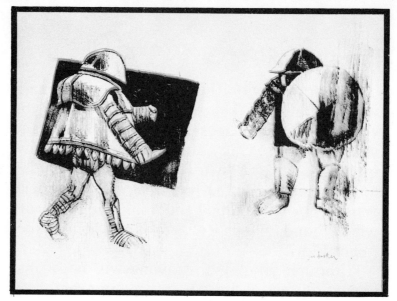

JOE LASKER

Drawing from Imagination

When you've had a little experience drawing people, you may want to make up some figures in various imaginary attitudes and actions. How would a trapeze artist look, and what would he be doing? What about drawing an acrobat, a football player, a ballet dancer, a colonel in the Czar's cavalry? When you work from imagination, you must try to visualize the special qualities of your subject.

Fashion and costume designers draw figures all the time, though their emphasis is on clothing and not on what the people are doing. You can rough in a figure for this kind of drawing with simple ovals and then proceed to dress it! Perhaps you can invent some exotic costumes. What would you wear to a costume party or a masquerade ball? Would you dress as a jockey, a tramp, a deep-sea diver, a knight in armor? Enliven your finished drawings with a touch of color.

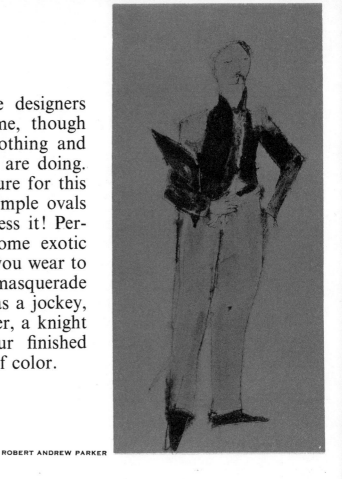

ROBERT ANDREW PARKER

Tones

A tone is a shade of black or a shade of color. When you use a tone combined with simple line, your drawing will look more solid and more interesting. Here is a way to make a figure drawing using tones. Get a small sponge, or a piece of sponge. (If you can't find a sponge, a crumpled-up facial tissue will do.) Pour two or three drops of ink onto a plate and add about two tablespoons of water. Mix the ink and water. Dip your sponge lightly into the mixture. Then press the sponge down lightly on a piece of scrap paper and quickly lift it straight up again. You'll see that the sponge leaves a large and pleasantly textured tone of gray.

Use the sponge to put the main masses of the figure on paper—a few big dabs for the body, some slimmer dabs (with the narrow part of the sponge) for the arms and legs. *Then* take your pencil, or pen and ink, and draw in the figure with lines. Try using colored ink, instead of black ink, for your tones. Or use water color, which is a transparent paint. The drawing in the lower right-hand corner of the page opposite was made with white paint sponged onto colored paper.

EDGAR DEGAS

ALPHONSE LEGROS

1526

VIVENTIS·POTVIT·DVRERIVS·ORA·PHILIPPI
MENTEM·NON·POTVIT·PINGERE·DOCTA
MANVS

ALBRECHT DÜRER

HENRI MATISSE

Drawing Heads

A person's face can tell you so much! It mirrors disappointment, surprise, pleasure. A face will tell you if a person is jolly or serious or sad. A face, then—a head—is always interesting to draw.

Each drawing on the page opposite has the special feeling of a particular person. The drawing in the upper left-hand corner of the page opposite, by Edgar Degas, captures the poise and grace of the ballet dancer he was sketching. The drawing by Matisse (lower right) shows the smooth, flowing lines and intricate patterns that the artist found most interesting.

Artists often draw portraits that look very much like the subject. The drawing by Albrecht Dürer (lower left) is probably an accurate portrait of somebody. (It was done in the sixteenth century, so you can't very well compare it with the subject.) However, in the heads you are about to draw, don't bother about a likeness. You can try portraits a little later on, after you've had some practice.

BEN SHAHN

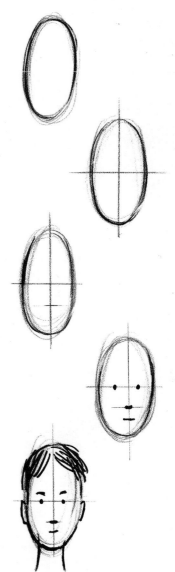

Before you can recognize and draw the special quality of a head, you must know where the features normally go. One person's idea of the average, typical head is illustrated above. It is a drawing made in the sixteenth century by Leonardo da Vinci. The ruled lines show how he divided it up into certain definite proportions.

You can make a similar "classic" head for yourself in the following way:

1.   Draw an oval.

2.   With light lines, divide the oval in half both horizontally and vertically.

3.   Divide the lower half of the vertical line in half again.

4.   Add a few dots and dashes, as illustrated, and you have a head with all its features in the typical position.

5.   Put in a few lines for hair, ears, and neck—and you have finished your "classic" head.

That was easy. But for a drawing that has any feeling and character, you will have to do more than make an oval and a few dots and dashes.

How to Draw a Head

Photographs of heads are reproduced on the page opposite, to show you how various features look. For your first few drawings, try mainly to place all the features. Remember, a likeness is not important.

1. Let's start with that big fellow wearing a hat, in the top left-hand photograph. Look for the basic shape of his head. It is a simple, broad oval. Pencil it in lightly.

2. Now think about the features. The nose is a good starting point. It's a sort of landmark. This fellow has a big, pudgy nose that could certainly be drawn as a simple U-shaped line.

3. Next come the eyes. An eye is often drawn as an oval with a circle inside. But it can be done in any number of other ways. You can make a black smudge, a simple dot, or a dash, or a circle.

4. As you work, think about the entire head, not just the part you are drawing at the moment. This will help you to fit all the parts together. The mouth has a lot to do with expression. If the corners of the mouth are turned down, you get a frown. If they are turned up, you get a smile. If you draw a circle, the mouth is open. You can draw our model's mouth with two wide arcs.

5. You can suggest the hat with three broad ovals, and the ears with simple loops. The chin and neck are round, fat curves. Most of the lines and shapes in this drawing are big and pudgy. This is the character of the man you are drawing, and this is the quality you want to get down on paper.

6. You can finish your drawing with the suggestion of shoulders and chest.

Take a careful look at what you have done, then put your drawing aside and try some of the other heads reproduced on page 30. Work as you did for the first drawing— looking for basic shapes and simple lines that will capture the character of your subject. If you do lots of heads, you'll find your work getting better and better.

When your drawings begin to look as if they might resemble actual people, you might try drawing someone you know. Get a friend or relative to pose for you.

There is one model who is always available. That is you! All you need is a good-sized mirror. Prop it up on your worktable, and you can draw yourself. Practically all artists have done self-portraits at one time or another. Rembrandt made dozens. He would paint his own picture whenever there was no one else available to pose for him.

PAUL CÉZANNE

How about making up some imaginary heads? How would a pirate look with a beard and mustache and a patch over one eye? How would a gangster look, or a beggar, or a man from Mars, or King Arthur? Can you make up a sad head, a silly head, a frightened head, a horrible head?

VINCENT VAN GOGH

BERNARD KARFIOL

Drawing Landscapes

If you tried to draw every leaf on a tree, or every grain of sand on a beach, your task would be impossible. You can't draw nature exactly as you see it. Nobody can. Only a camera copies precisely what it sees.

The artist's job is to make a picture that shows how he thinks and feels about his subject. He may try to tell in his drawing how it *feels* to be in a grassy meadow, or he may try to capture the wetness of a rainstorm, but he does not draw every single blade of grass or every drop of rain.

The drawing by Vincent van Gogh opposite is a good example of how an artist will change and simplify his subject matter to suit himself. No cypress tree ever looked like the one Van Gogh drew. But he evidently found the spiraling, flamelike foliage of the cypress very appealing, and this quality is apparent in every part of his drawing. Another artist might have reacted to the very same tree by drawing an altogether different picture.

A drawing is a personal expression in which the subject may be changed, rearranged, simplified, or turned topsy-turvy to suit the artist.

LEONARDO DA VINCI

Paris. 1924.

MAURICE UTRILLO

How To Draw A Landscape

Look at the photograph reproduced above. Pretend you are sitting under a shady oak on a hilltop; directly before you lies a peaceful valley with trees and neighboring mountains, and you also see a little hilltop town. If you work from

this photograph, you will be able to follow, step by step, a systematic way of doing a landscape drawing with wash.

Wash is ink (or black water-color paint) mixed with water. The more water you add to the black, the lighter the tones. Wash is a way of getting a rich variety of soft grays. Its name comes from the manner in which the tone is applied. It is "washed" onto the paper with a large soft water-color brush. It is usually brushed on very freely and loosely.

MATERIALS: You will need pen and ink (India ink is best), pencil, a large soft water-color brush, two or three small dishes in which to mix your washes, and paper. The paper should be quite heavy, so that it will not wrinkle when you put the wash on. Use a smooth water-color paper or Bristol board.

You approach a landscape in the same way as your other drawings. Look for the main shapes and forms. What interests you especially? Do you want to concentrate on the tree in the foreground, or on the little hilltop houses, or perhaps on the mountains in the background? Is there something you want to change, or add, or leave out?

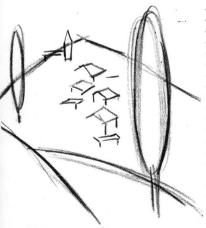

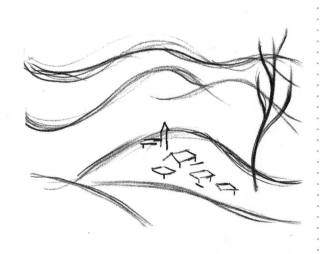

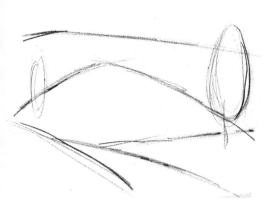

1. First pencil in the main forms very lightly. One main form is the mountains, another the hill with the town, another the large tree on the right, still another the road in the foreground. When you pencil in the main shapes, you are *composing* your picture. The way you combine the lines and shapes of your picture—and the way you arrange them on paper—is called composition. There are three drawings on the page opposite, all from the same photograph. Each is composed in a different way.

2. Now for the wash. Put two or three drops of ink on a plate. Or put some black water color on a plate. Then add three or four tablespoons of water and stir the mixture with your brush. If you want a lighter gray, use more water. Start with a light tone. You can always darken a light gray by adding more wash—later on in your drawing— but you can't make a dark tone any lighter once it has been brushed onto the paper.

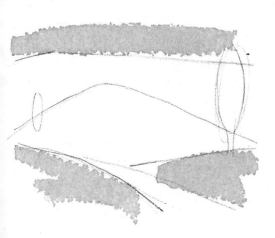

3. When you have mixed the wash, brush in a tone wherever you feel you need it— perhaps in the sky, or the mountains in the background, or the road or tree in the foreground. The area covered with wash will immediately become separate from the rest of your drawing.

4. Give the wash a few minutes to dry. Then if you think it should be darker, add some more wash. Don't draw lines with the wash. Do that later with your pen and ink.

5. Once all the tones are in, you can begin to draw with pen and ink. If you draw over a part of the paper that is wet, the ink will run. This can look pleasing; but when you don't want the ink to run, you must let the wash dry completely.

6. There are a great many small houses, trees, and shrubs in this landscape. Don't feel that you have to include everything. You can eliminate whatever seems too cluttered, or unclear, or unimportant.

7. Pen and ink are good for suggesting texture. There are many different textures in this landscape; use them to give your drawing some variety. The foreground and the foliage of the tree, for instance, would be enriched by a little texture.

8. When you finish the pen-and-ink part of the drawing, you may want to go back and add some more wash—perhaps a deep shadow here and there, or an accent, or a slightly darker tone somewhere.

WILLEM VAN DE VELDE

JOE LASKER

LEONARDO DA VINCI

PAUL KLEE

Try another drawing from the same photograph. Compose your picture differently and put your washes in different places. See what varying effects you can get. Try a drawing without the wash. You learn a great deal by drawing one subject several times and by doing it differently each time.

Now that you've tried a landscape, go out and sketch some of the neighboring countryside. Is there a park or a lake in your neighborhood? What about drawing a city landscape? Can you draw what you see from your window?

Try using color, instead of black, to make your wash. This will really brighten up a drawing. Make sure that you use transparent water color, and not a heavy tempera or poster color.

MAURICE SENDAK

Showing Space

How do you make a building look solid? When you draw the floor in a room, how do you make it look like a floor and not a wall? How do you show that something is far away—or close? These questions are answered by the rules of perspective. Perspective is the technique of getting an object to look correctly in place when drawn on paper. There are five basic rules:

1. A basic principle of perspective is that things look large when close and small when far away. For example, if you look at a row of telephone poles, you will see that they seem to get smaller as they get farther away.

2. Objects close to you usually appear darker and more vivid than objects in the distance. Have you ever stood on a hilltop (or looked out the window of a tall building) and noticed how houses or mountains far away seem hazy and vague, whereas a tree or roof close by is sharp and clear?

3. Objects close to you will overlap whatever happens to be behind them. For example, in the drawing on the left, the glass is farther away than the bottle. Therefore the bottle overlaps the glass.

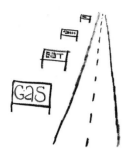

4. Objects that are far away from you usually appear higher up than objects close to you. For example, a road gets higher and higher as it recedes into the distance. (It also gets smaller and smaller, as the first rule of perspective explains.)

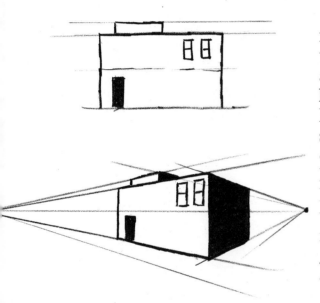

5. Parallel lines appear to come together far away, at the horizon. For example, the top and bottom lines of a building are actually parallel. This is apparent when you look at the building from directly in front. But when you see it from an angle, the lines seem to come closer together at the far end of the building. And if you extended these lines (or if the building were a hundred miles long), they would seem to come together at the horizon. Have you ever noticed how railroad tracks come closer together as they go toward the horizon? The same principle applies here.

NUREMBERG CHRONICLES

Artists didn't know the principles of perspective until the time of the Italian Renaissance (about 1500). Drawings and paintings done before that time often tend to have a flat and somewhat strange, unreal look.

Today many artists intentionally ignore perspective. They feel they can best express feeling or mood and emotion by means of shapes and lines and colors. They would rather do this than make a realistic picture using the principles of perspective.

WILLIAM GLACKENS

MAURICE SENDAK

REMBRANDT VAN RIJN

Drawing Scenes

So far we've discussed one-at-a-time subjects such as animals, figures, heads, and landscapes. When a number of these subjects are combined, you have a scene. A scene usually contains one or more figures in some sort of setting, and there is usually some action. Sometimes scenes are called illustrations—they illustrate or describe an event.

Because scenes contain many different elements, they can become quite complicated. The scene by Rembrandt, at the top of this page, shows crowds of people, violent activity. But all of it hangs together well, and the final effect is one of great dramatic intensity. Can you see why some parts of the drawing are light, others dark?

How to Draw a Scene

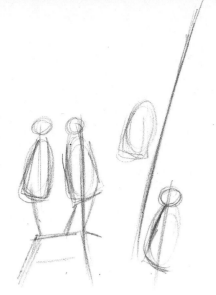

1. Here's a photograph of a scene that is filled with action and excitement. After you've studied it for a few moments, pencil in the main shapes very lightly. This is your "map"—to show where everything belongs.

2. Now draw the two figures on the left, and the platform on which they are standing. (You can do this either in pencil or in pen and ink.) When you draw the figures, look for the action lines. Don't fuss with all the little folds and wrinkles in the raincoats.

3. Next draw the fireman in the right foreground. In drawing this fellow, shift him a bit to the right so that he won't block from view the figures climbing the ladder. Artists often make this type of change to simplify a drawing. Most things are too complicated to draw exactly as they appear.

4. Now draw the ladder with the men climbing it. These figures are small and bulky, but you'll be able to draw them if you first puzzle out the action lines.

5. Now you are ready for some of the details—the railings, the hoses, the pipes, the rungs of the ladder. Don't clutter your drawing with everything you see in the photograph. You would do well to leave out some of that complicated bracing on the ladder.

6. A fire is exciting! Is there any way to make your drawing more exciting? How about smoke? There is plenty in the photograph, but it looks like fog or clouds. Draw some real black, dangerous-looking smoke! How about flames? How about someone leaning way out of a window and crying loudly for help?

One way to make a drawing dramatic is to contrast light and dark areas with one another. Try this scene again, using wash and pen and ink. See if you can create a feeling of excitement by using the wash to make strong contrasts of light and dark.

There are other ways, besides wash, to get dark tones. Crosshatching with pen and ink is one good method. Crosshatching consists of many parallel lines drawn close together at different angles. The illustration below shows some of the many ways of getting dark tones with pen and ink.

EUGENE BERMAN

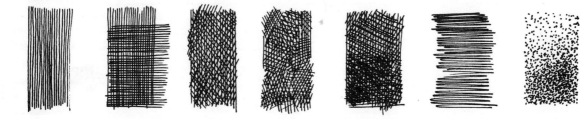

Draw this fire scene several times, but vary it each time. Shift some of the figures about, or add some more firemen and ladders, or change the size of your drawing. You'll learn a great deal by doing many different drawings of the very same scene.

Then you can look for other scenes. Picture ideas don't always come easily; you must form the habit of looking for them. Perhaps you will see something at home, or in the street, that provides good material for a picture. Have you been to the circus or the rodeo recently? Have you read a story or seen a television play that suggests a good picture? How about an imaginary scene . . . a train crash, the dramatic moment of a ballet, six men at work inside a submarine. Can you think of an interesting scene to draw?

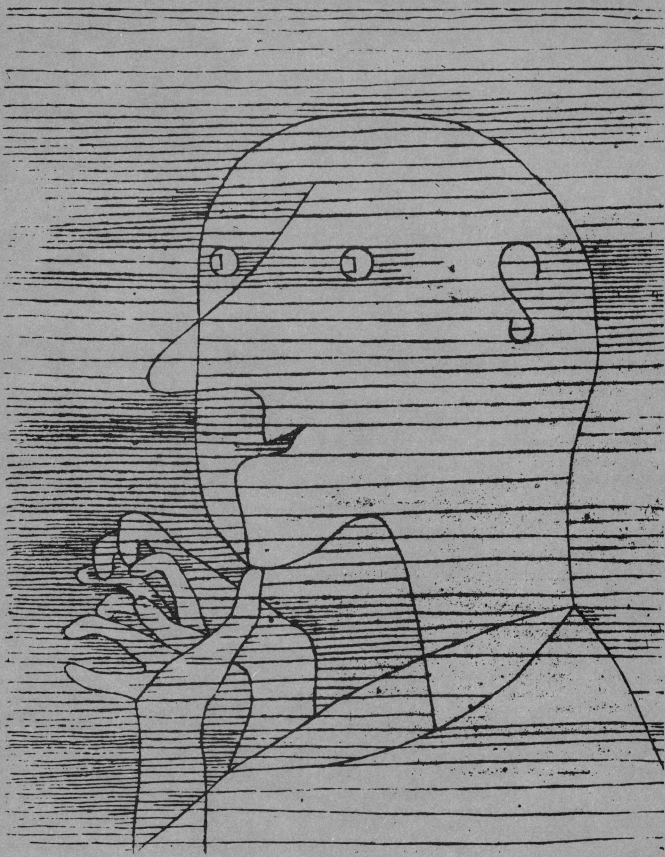

PAUL KLEE

Experimenting with Pencil, Pen, and Brush

Life would be dull if you always did the same thing in the same way. This is true of drawing too. If you want to stay interested and if you want to keep improving, you have to try different approaches, and different materials, and different ideas.

So far we have tried pencil, pen and ink, wash, and a few other drawing techniques. This section discusses some more ideas, some other ways of working with which you may want to experiment from time to time.

PAVEL TCHELITCHEW

HANS ARP

ALBERT ALCALAY

Lines, Shapes, and Abstract Drawings

This book has been concerned with animals, people, places—things that already exist. But an artist can make drawings that have no real subject at all—drawings that are simply combinations of lines, tones, textures, and shapes.

Suppose you wanted to draw a design. Perhaps you saw a flying bird and liked the lines formed by its wings. You might decide not to draw the rest of the bird, but just to make a design based on these lines. You could start your drawing with these lines and then continue, adding varied lines, shapes, tones, and textures as you saw fit, to get a lively, interesting design. You might try to capture the feeling of flying in your drawing. Your finished drawing could turn out to be quite elaborate without even resembling the original bird that you saw.

If you worked in this way, you would be making an abstract drawing. And this is just the sort of drawing that many modern artists find most interesting.

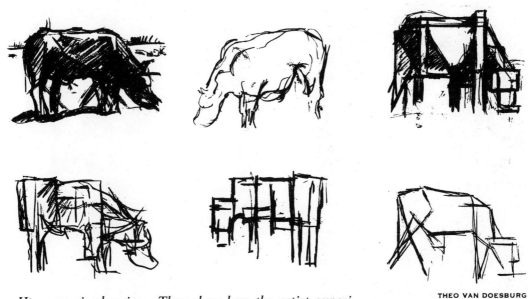

THEO VAN DOESBURG

Here are six drawings. They show how the artist experimented in an effort to find the most interesting lines and shapes in a cow. Some of the drawings are realistic—others quite abstract.

Exaggeration

Exaggeration is one way of making things dramatic. If you say that someone is as tall as a tree, you are exaggerating. No one is really that tall. You can use the same sort of overstatement in drawing to emphasize or dramatize an idea.

Suppose, for example, you make a drawing of someone who is always eavesdropping. You might draw ears as big as his head. No one's ears are that big. This would be exaggeration used to dramatize the idea that the person is an eavesdropper.

Or if—in drawing a head—you make your subject's pointy nose look like a needle, you are exaggerating in order to draw attention to this special-looking nose. Exaggerated drawings can be very funny. They are sometimes called caricatures. (The dividing line between a cartoon caricature and a fine artist's exaggeration is sometimes pretty thin.)

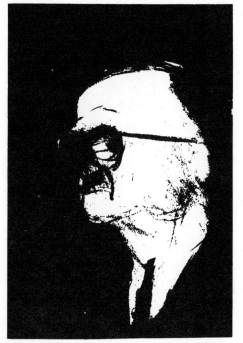

JOE LASKER

LEONARDO DA VINCI

56

Sometimes an artist will make extreme distortions in order to give the strongest possible impression of something. The mural *Guernica*, by Pablo Picasso (reproduced below), is distorted and exaggerated in order to show most dramatically the ruins and horror of a bombed-out town. Guernica, a town in Spain, was completely destroyed by fascist bombers in 1937.

GEORGE GROSZ

PABLO PICASSO

LINE DRAWING

JOE LASKER

Drawing without Line

Most drawings in this book are done with simple line. The line is used to show the outline, or contour, of the shape you are drawing. But it is also possible to draw the area, or shape, without line.

In order to do this, you need something like the brush and wash, or the sponge described on page 24. Charcoal and Conté crayon are also good for roughing in large areas of tone.

Charcoal, which is burnt wood, can be bought at any art store. Conté (a nongreasy crayon) is also available there, and in several colors. These age-old materials were used by such artists as Michelangelo and Leonardo da Vinci. Get some special charcoal paper, which is best suited for charcoal and Conté. It has a slightly rough texture. A large sheet costs just a few cents, and it comes in many handsome colors.

If you take a small piece of charcoal or Conté and hold it on its side you can, quickly and in one motion, make a large, flat, even tone. For a sharp line, use the edge of the charcoal or Conté.

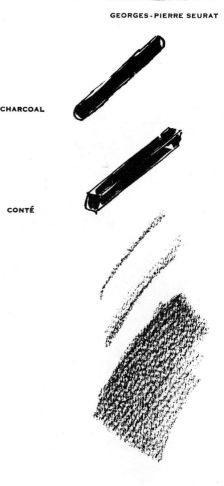

TONE DRAWING

GEORGES-PIERRE SEURAT

CHARCOAL

CONTÉ

You will find it interesting to use red or brown Conté crayon to rough in the big forms in a drawing. Then, if you want detail, go back over the drawing with pen and ink for outlines and accents. The rough colored crayon and the firm black line create a beautiful contrast.

After using charcoal, spray your finished drawing with fixative. Fixative—a thin, transparent lacquer or varnish available in art stores—is used to protect charcoal and pastel drawings so that they won't smudge.

GEORGES-PIERRE SEURAT

HERBERT MESIBOV

Spatter

Spatter is another interesting way of working. A spray of ink or paint is added to a drawing for the sake of tone or texture. The easiest way to spatter is to put a few drops of ink on the bristle tips of an old toothbrush. Hold the brush as illustrated below and draw your finger back toward you—away from the end of the toothbrush. As you do this, a fine spray or spatter of ink will be thrown off. With a little practice, you'll be able to direct the spray fairly accurately.

If you want the spatter to appear only in certain areas, "mask off" the section you want to protect. Use pieces of cardboard to cover the parts of the drawing you do not want to spatter.

Or, take a sheet of heavy paper and cut out of it the shapes that are supposed to receive a tone. Place this cut-out paper over your drawing to control the spatter.

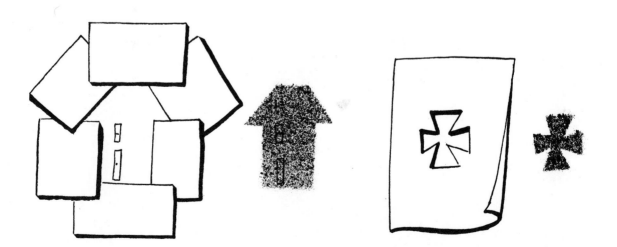

You can use spatter on a finished drawing, or you can use it as a background before you even start to draw. If you have some colored ink, try beginning a picture with spatter.

Toulouse-Lautrec was probably the first artist to make much use of this technique. One of the lithographs in which Toulouse-Lautrec used spatter is reproduced below.

HENRI DE TOULOUSE-LAUTREC

Contrast

Contrast helps to make a drawing interesting. For example, a picture of a long, monotonous row of houses would be pretty dull if all the houses were exactly alike.

But if some of the houses were made dark and others light, there would be a contrast and the drawing would appear much more lively.

And if the houses had textures that contrasted with one another, the drawing would become still more interesting.

There are many other ways of getting contrast. You could make some of the houses larger than others. You could add color in some areas. You might also vary the quality of the line you use—light, heavy, jiggly, fuzzy. Or you might add a figure in the foreground or clouds in the sky. An artist often changes and shifts his subject about simply for the sake of giving his drawing contrast.

Anatomy

After you've drawn animals and people for a while, you may feel that your work would improve if you knew something about bones and muscles. Anatomy is the study of the parts of a body—how these parts fit together and how they work. Any number of excellent anatomy books have been designed specifically for the artist, and these will prove helpful.

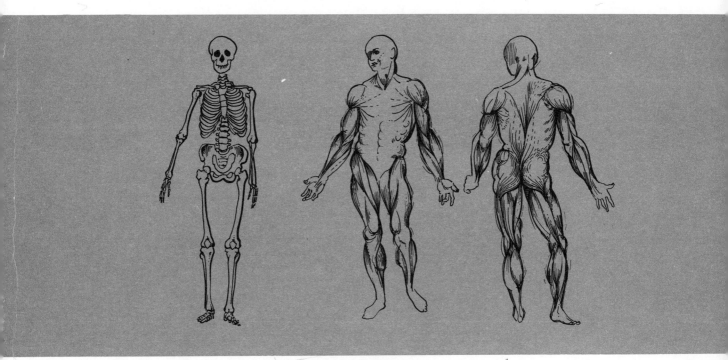

Other Books about Drawing

There is one book on drawing which this author finds immeasurably superior to others. It is *The Natural Way to Draw*, a working plan for art study, by Kimon Nicolaides, published by the Houghton Mifflin Company, Boston. It belongs on every artist's bookshelf.

There are, of course, many books on special aspects of drawing, such as mechanical drawing, commercial illustration, pencil techniques, and so on. Books of this sort are to be found in most libraries.

About the Illustrations

EDGAR DEGAS

Books in the Beginning Artist's Series
by Harvey Weiss

SCULPTURE: *Clay, Wood and Wire*

PRINTMAKING: *Paper, Ink and Roller*

DRAWING: *Pencil, Pen and Brush*

CRAFTS: *Sticks, Spools and Feathers*

POTTERY: *Ceramics: From Clay to Kiln*

PAINTING: *Paint, Brush and Palette*

CRAFTS: *Collage and Construction*

PHOTOGRAPHY: *Lens and Shutter*

FILMMAKING: *How to Make Your Own Movies*

C -3

CLAY, WOOD and WIRE

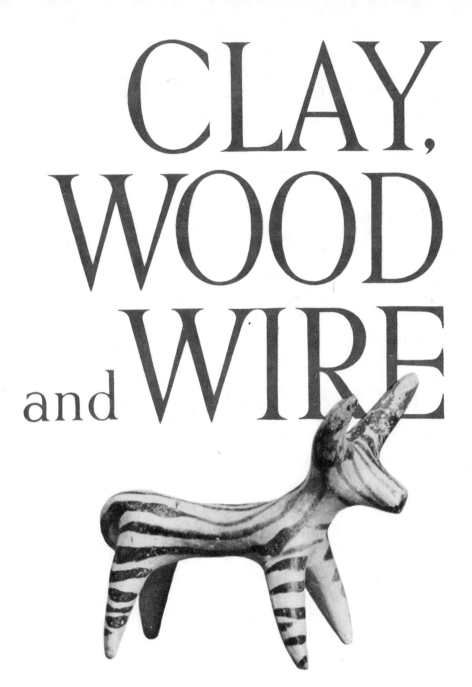

A HOW-TO-DO-IT BOOK OF SCULPTURE

By Harvey Weiss

YOUNG SCOTT BOOKS

Table Of Contents

Thanks and acknowledgment are due the following museums, institutions, and individuals for their cooperation and generous help in the preparation of this book: The Museum of Modern Art, New York; The American Museum of Natural History, New York; The Metropolitan Museum of Art, New York; The Rhode Island School of Design Museum, Providence, Rhode Island; The Cleveland Art Institute, Cleveland, Ohio; The Boston Museum of Fine Arts, Boston, Massachusetts; The Old Dartmouth Historical and Whaling Museum, New Bedford, Massachusetts; Soprintendenza Antichita, Firenze, Italy; Washington University, St. Louis, Missouri; The Des Moines Art Center, Des Moines, Iowa; The Canadian Department of Northern Affairs and National Resources, Ottawa; Mr. Bert Beaver; Miss Dorothea Denislow of the Sculpture Center, New York; Mr. Glen Chamberlain; Miss Kate Bernhardt; May, Bill, John, and especially my wife, Miriam.

This is a book about sculpture. It's about how to make lions, and horses, and heads, and figures running, and designs that can hang and twirl. It's about pipe-cleaners, and clay, and cardboard, and plasticene, and plaster. It's about all sorts of things that are easy to make if you know how to go about it.

It shows you how other people have made sculpture, and it will show you how to get started making your own sculpture out of many different materials.

c.

d.

g.

HORSES

Here are horses—six of them—galloping, prancing, or just standing still. Some are small and simple, some are big and complicated. They are six horses made the way six different artists felt like making a horse. No one horse is more "right" or "correct" than any other. They are just different. They are different because each artist had his own special feeling about a horse. But notice that even the ones that are very simple and uncomplicated have the lively, prancing, galloping feeling of a horse.

What's your way to make a horse? How would you do it? Do you like the nice thin legs? Or would you concentrate on the big round, galloping body with a long neck and a flowing mane? Or maybe you're especially fond of lazy horses munching grass or a horse prancing in a parade.

These are things for you to decide, because now *you're* the artist.

The next few pages show you how to make a horse out of a material that's very easy to manage. With pipe-cleaners it's the easiest thing in the world. Here's how you do it . . .

e.

h.

i.

6

How To Make A Horse Out Of Pipe-Cleaners

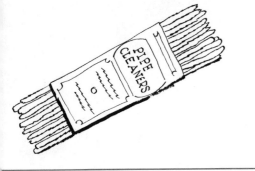

1. The first thing you need is a handful of pipe-cleaners. You can get them in any cigar store, or, if you know someone who smokes a pipe, he'll have some.

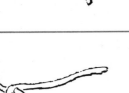

2. Make the hind legs first. Just take one cleaner and bend it in the middle.

3. Now take another cleaner and twist it around the hind legs. Let a little bit stick out for the tail.

4. Twist on another cleaner for the front legs. Then put on another for the neck and head.

5. Cut off a small piece and wrap it around the head. If you let the ends stick up a little, you will have the ears. At this point the horse can stand on its own four feet and should begin to look something like a horse. Now is the time for you to decide just how you want it to look—fat, skinny, tired, galloping, sitting, munching lunch? That's up to you. It's your horse.

6. If you want the body a little fatter, take more pipe-cleaners and wrap them around the body between the front and back legs.

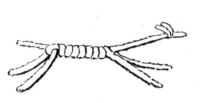

7. One of the nice things about making your horse out of pipe-cleaners is that, once he's all put together, you can try different things with him. Try spreading his feet apart and see if you can make him look as if he's running fast. Make the head and neck stretch forward, and he'll look as if he were really dashing along. Notice how the straight line of the back and the neck helps to give him a feeling of speed.

8. See if you can make your horse have the feeling of trotting. Then his neck will be up, straight and proud. How about lifting one of his feet up in the air and making his tail stick up? He'll seem to prance along.

9. Maybe you'd like to put a rider on his back. If you do, you'll need four more pipe-cleaners. Take one and bend it in the middle. This will be the legs.

10. Take another and bend the top a half-inch down. This will be the head and body. Fasten it to the legs.

11. Twist on another piece, just below the head, for the arms. And wrap still another around the body to make it a little heavier.

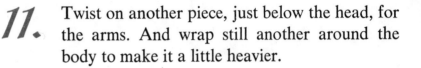

12. Put the man on the horse's back. If the horse is racing, you'll probably want the rider leaning forward, holding the reins. (You can make the reins out of some heavy thread.)

13. There are lots of things you can do with your horse and rider. See what other actions you can discover. Don't be afraid to bend and twist and turn and experiment. When you decide that you're all finished, you can cut out a piece of cardboard and cement the horse's feet to it. This will be the base and will keep the horse from being knocked over.

You can make all sorts of other animals or figures out of pipe-cleaners. What about a dinosaur? Or two people running? Or a big-eared donkey pulling a wagon? Or a leopard? (You can paint spots on him.) Or a giraffe with a long thin neck? Or an octopus with twelve arms all painted black? You can make a whole zoo full of animals, or a farm, or a rodeo of cowpunchers with lassos. It's up to you.

a.

b.

c.

f.

LIONS

Lions are fun to make. Look at these. They're strong and exciting and handsome. They have a fierce, king-of-the-jungle look.

They don't all look exactly like the lions you see in the zoo, but these are *sculpture*-lions. A sculpture lion can give the *feeling* of a real lion, even if he doesn't look too much like a real lion. Sometimes just a few lumps of clay put together in the right way will do the trick. You can suggest the roar without every whisker being there. A statue doesn't have to be fussy or real-looking to get the feeling of a lion.

You can make a lion. It's not much harder than the horse.

What do you want your lion to look like? Do you want him to look fierce? Maybe you'd prefer a friendly little baby lion to a fierce roaring one. Or maybe your fierce lion will end up looking more like a house cat or a shaggy poodle. In that case there's no reason why you can't just pretend that's what you wanted to make in the first place! (Nobody will ever know.)

You can't always get just what you want the first time you try, but if *you* like the way it comes out—then you're doing all right.

How To Make A Lion Out Of Plasticene

1. First get some plasticene. (You can get it in any art store.) Plasticene is a kind of clay that never dries up. It is strong and easy to manage, and you can use it over and over again.

2. To start your lion, you need a flat piece of wood for a base. A heavy piece of cardboard will do if you can't get wood. About 4 x 6 inches is a good size.

3. Make four balls of plasticene. These will be the legs. You'll find that the plasticene is hard and stiff if you use big lumps of it, but if you break off little pieces and squeeze them in your fingers a few times they will become soft and workable.

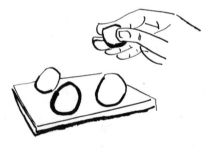

4. Make another, larger, longer ball and put it on top of the four legs. This will be the body. Make sure the legs are squeezed firmly into the body.

5. Then make another large oval ball for the head. Squeeze it on good and tight, or it may fall off later.

6. Here the fun begins. You have somewhat the shape of a lion. Now push and poke and squeeze and pinch. Add plasticene or take it away. Keep at it until your lion begins to look the way you want it to. Be bold. Get the graceful "sweep" of the back. Get the powerful, round chest and big, proud head. At first it may not look like a lion to anyone but you. But take your time about it, and keep trying until you begin to get what you want.

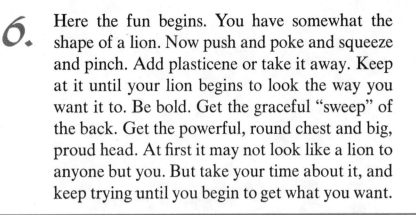

7. You are making a lion, and the thing about lions is that they roar. So let's make him roar. Just scoop out a big mouth. Put in his teeth. Now is he roaring? If you were making a hippopotamus instead of a lion, you would make him big and round and lumpy and heavy. If you were making a snake, you would make him thin and wriggly and squiggly. If you were making a wart hog, you would make him wrinkled and bumpy and warty and ugly. Every animal has some one special thing you will want to emphasize.

8. Last of all put in the smaller details, like eyes and ears and paws and tail. You can make the eyes just by poking a couple of holes in the head with the point of a pencil. A little ball of plasticene can make the nose. You can make the lion's mane with thin strips of plasticene stuck on, one on top of the other, all around the head.

9. When you think you're through with your lion, try holding him up against a strong light and look to see if he has a clean, definite outline or silhouette. Look at him from all sides. If he is bumpy and unsure, work on him some more.

If you feel that you would rather make your lion some other way—do it. Maybe you would rather have him sitting down, or yawning, or all curled up sleeping.

Or maybe you'd rather make an elephant, or an airplane, or a tugboat, or a kangaroo with a baby in its pouch, or a tiny mouse with big ears and a long tail.

If you like, you can make the lion out of clay instead of plasticene. But if you do, read the next chapter first, so you will know how to handle the clay.

a.

b.

c.

e.

14

h.

HEADS

Big eyes or little eyes? Curly hair, big chin, pointy chin, small ears, stubby nose or long nose? That's what heads are made of, and that's what makes one head different from another.

Sometimes just a few scratches in the clay will suggest these things and give the whole feeling and mood of a head.

Look at that fellow above and to the left. He's made up of a few simple shapes, but they tell a lot. One hand is raised to his head. His eyes are big and startled. He could be about to say, "Oh, what an awful headache I've got," or, "Gosh, why didn't I think of that!"

Some of these heads look like someone in particular, and are called "portraits." Others are just for fun. Maybe the artist felt like making a head with big ears and a fancy hat. Or maybe he decided he would make a head with round smooth shapes that are nice to touch. Perhaps he wanted to show how happy a friend looks when he laughs.

Sometimes a dot with a sharp tool will look like an eye, or a lump of clay will make a nose. A line scratched in the clay can make a fine mouth.

g.

i.

j.

k.

How To Make A Head Out Of Clay

Clay is used for sculpture more often than any other material. You can squeeze and push and form it like plasticene, but, when it dries, it is quite hard. If you want it still harder, you can bake it in a special, very hot oven called a "kiln." This baking is called "firing." After it is fired, the clay is called "terra cotta," which is Latin for "cooked earth." Special colors, called "glazes," can be baked onto the clay, or it can be painted with ordinary paints.

Many schools have kilns for firing clay. And potters and brickmakers also have kilns. If you ask around in your neighborhood, the chances are you'll find there's a kiln nearby where you can take your finished things to be fired.

Another possibility is to use one of the special clays which can be fired in a kitchen oven. And then there is still another kind of clay, called "self-hardening," which dries hard as a rock without any firing at all.

But even if you can't locate a kiln or get these special clays, regular clay is all right. You'll just have to handle the finished pieces a little more gently.

1. To start making a head get some clay from an art store. Find a small square board and put a nail in the center of it. This will keep the clay from falling over.

2. Then squeeze and squish the clay until it is easy to handle. (This will also work out the air bubbles that would cause trouble later if you are going to fire your piece.) If the clay seems too stiff and hard, or if it cracks when you bend it, it is probably too dry. Sprinkle a little water on it.

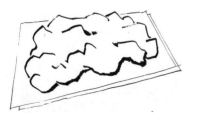

3. If the clay is soft and mushy, it is too wet. Spread it out on a newspaper for a few minutes and let it dry a bit.

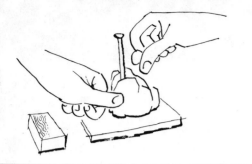

4. Start by putting clay, bit by bit, around and above the nail. Slowly and carefully build up the shape you want. Concentrate on getting the rough general shape of the head first.

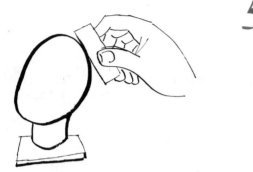

5. Most people's heads are shaped like an egg, but make the head the way you want it. Maybe you want a square head or a perfectly round one. Whatever you do, make it a definite shape, not a wishy-washy one. A block of wood is a handy tool to use for "tapping" the clay into the shapes you want.

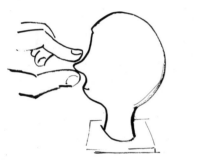

6. When you are satisfied with the shape of the head, *then* start on the details like eyes, mouth, hair. You may be able to "pinch out" some of these shapes from the larger mass.

7. The mouth can be a simple straight line scratched under the nose. The eyes can be a couple of large dots, and a little roll of clay placed above them will make the eyebrows.

8. Two small flaps of clay will make the ears. And the hair will look best if you try to get the rough general shapes rather than a lot of tiny, scratchy strands of hair.

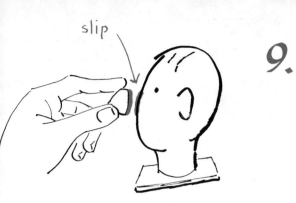

slip

9. You may find it easier to add on separate parts like nose, or ears, or a hat. When you add separate parts, first take a little clay and water and mix them until the clay becomes quite mushy. This mushy clay is called "slip," and it will act as a sort of cement that will help the parts stick together. Whenever you want to join two pieces of clay, spread a layer of slip over both parts where they join. Then squeeze them together hard. If you don't, they may fall apart when the clay dries out.

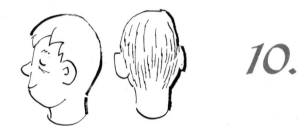

10. Keep turning the head around as you work on it, so that you see it from all sides. Keep the parts simple and forget about all the little bumps and wrinkles and freckles.

11. When the head is finished you can take it off the wooden base. If you turn it upside down and scoop out some of the clay from the inside with a spoon or a wire tool, it will be easier to fire.

12. After the clay is completely dry, it can be painted or fired.

Try making different kinds of heads. You can make an old man in a hat, a little girl with lots of curly hair. Or how about the head of a dog, or a cat, or a rhinoceros?

If the head you make doesn't look like any of the pictures in the book, never mind. It shouldn't. Everybody makes things his own way. If *you* like it, it's good!

a.

b.

c.

d.

20

e.

f.

FIGURES

Here are figures that were made in many places and in many different times. That fellow playing the harp was made by an artist on an island in the Mediterranean four thousand years before Columbus discovered America. The dancers were made in France only forty or fifty years ago. The sad-looking man holding his head was found in Mexico. Nobody knows for sure just when it was made.

But all these figures have one thing in common. They are simple and they are bold. In the figure that you make, this is the thing to try for.

Look at how strong that Eskimo is! He's just a few simple, round shapes, and yet he really looks as if he's tugging away.

And the two men running—there's nothing fussy or tricky about them. They just have the bouncy, stretching feeling of running.

Making a figure out of clay is a little more difficult than making a head. But, if you take your time and follow the directions, it should turn out the way you want it to.

Here's how to do it.

k.

g.   h.   i.   j.

l.

m.

n.

o.

p.

How To Make A Figure

1. One way of making a figure is by putting together balls of clay—a big one for the body, a small round one for the head, four long ones for the arms and legs. This is very much like the way you put the plasticene lion together, earlier in the book.

2. Another good way to start is with a "stick figure." It's the same sort of figure you can draw with a pencil or crayon on paper, only now you're using clay. Make rolls of clay and put them together in the shape of a figure. Be sure that all the parts are joined firmly together. This is important. Use a little very mushy clay ("slip") as a cement and squeeze the parts hard into one another.

3. Now, decide just what kind of figure you want to make. Experiment with the stick figure. Try shifting and twisting and bending it in different positions until you find one you like. (If you make your figure sitting or kneeling or lying down it will be much easier.)

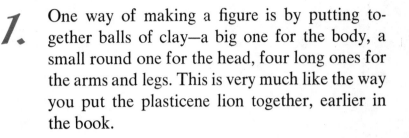

4. If you decide you want to make a clown standing with his hands on his hips, for example, this is what you do. Get a piece of wood for a base and press the feet onto it. Try to make the figure stand up by itself. If you made the clay rolls too thin, you will find that the figure will sag. In that case, add more clay, bit by bit, until it stands up by itself. You'll probably have to make very thick and heavy legs. Always bear in mind that clay is *not* a good material for making light, thin shapes. They are sure to break off when the clay dries out.

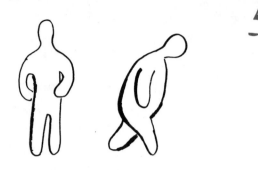

5. After you have your clown standing up, add more clay, a piece at a time, getting the shapes just the way you want them. Keep thinking of how you want the clown to look. If you make shapes that are straight and bold and strong, then the clown will have the feeling of strength and boldness. If you make shapes that are bent-over and droopy and sad, then your clown will look droopy and sad. The way you shape the clay will give your clown his own special look.

6. Try twisting his head in different directions. You can make him look up, down, or to the side. And how about his arms? There are many different ways to place them besides on the hips. And his legs—they can be bent, straight, twisted, spread apart, bowlegged, or even knock-kneed.

7. After you have all the big main shapes in place, put in the details. Don't put in so many that the figure is all cluttered up. Try a big nose that you can paint a bright red when the clay is dried out or fired. How about a funny hat? And what about great big, floppy shoes?

8. If you want to get a slightly different look in some places, try scratching or scraping the clay with a knife or a modeling tool. Or roll up little balls of clay and press them into place.

Try making some other figures. How about an acrobat standing on his head? Or a figure about to throw a basketball? Or two people wrestling? Or you might want to try making a figure by starting with a solid lump of clay and then taking away pieces until you get the figure you want. This is really a sort of carving.

Building A Figure On An Armature

1. If you want to make a figure that isn't blocky and solid-looking, you would do better to use plasticene instead of clay. Use it over some kind of skeleton or "armature." An armature will keep the figure from falling over. You can make one out of soft copper wire, nailed or thumb-tacked to the base. Make the armature like a stick figure. Adjust it to the position you want. Then fasten it to the base.

2. Put the plasticene on, bit by bit, over the wire. Build up the shapes you want in the same way as with clay.

3. You can make a wire armature for animals as well as for figures. It's a little like making the horse out of pipe-cleaners, except that now you're using copper wire. If you are going to make a giraffe, for example, the best way to keep the long, long thin neck and spindly legs from collapsing is to use an armature. It's up to you to decide when you need an armature.

MOBILES

A sculpture that moves is called a "mobile." A mobile is a combination of carefully-balanced shapes that hang from the ceiling. The slightest draft will set them spinning and turning and jiggling. As the mobile moves, its different parts move into different designs. It is always changing.

A mobile isn't usually made to look like anything in life. You are not apt to make mobiles that look like faces or figures, although you could. Instead, the interesting thing about mobiles is their design, their ever-changing quality, and the shadows that they cast.

The old Greek and Roman sculptors never heard of a mobile. In fact, nobody did until twenty or thirty years ago. It's a new type of sculpture that was first made by an American artist by the name of Alexander Calder.

All you need in order to make one are some pieces of cardboard, some stiff wire, a pair of pliers, and some string.

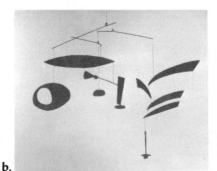

b.

How To Make A Mobile

The important thing about a mobile is to make it hang so that it balances. This isn't as easy as it looks.

1. Start out with a stiff piece of wire bent as in the picture. (Instead of wire, you can use a dowel, which is a thin wooden rod, or even a sturdy twig from a tree.)

2. Hang the first piece from a doorway with a piece of string. A thumb-tack or a small nail will hold it.

3. Tie on another piece of wire, or two, or three. Every time you add something, the balance will change, because it will put what you already have done out of balance. Then you will have to add something else somewhere else to get it back in balance again.

28

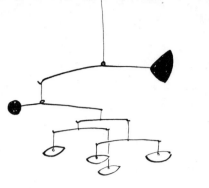

4. Try cutting cardboard into shapes you like, painting them, and then tieing them on.

5. Feathers are fun to put on. And what about pebbles, or cellophane in bright colors, paper clips, ribbons? Almost anything light in weight can be put on a mobile. But before you add everything in sight, stop to think how it will look. Too little is often better than too much.

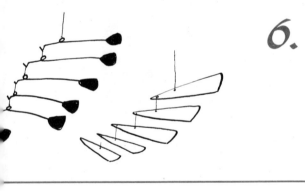

6. Try different types and combinations of balancing, and don't get discouraged if you have to do it over and over until you get it just right. If there is a part you don't like, then take it off and make something different to go in its place.

7. When you are satisfied that your mobile is as handsome as you can make it, then hang it from the ceiling in the middle of your room. You can tie it to a light fixture, for example, or tack it to the top of a window or doorway—any place where it can hang freely will do. Watch it move. Blow at it and see how it swings. Notice the shadows that it casts. That's half the fun.

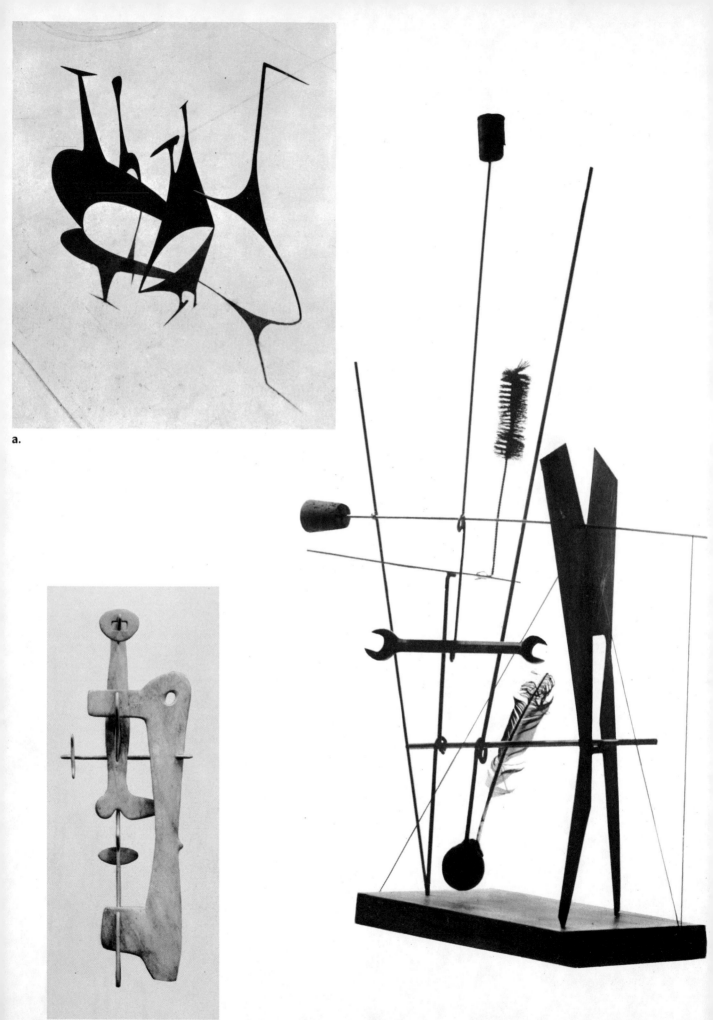

a.

b.

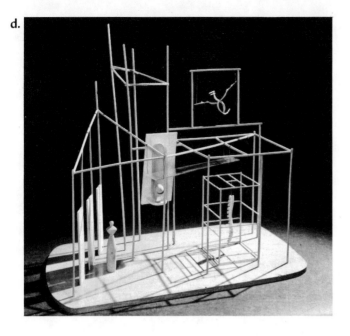

d.

CONSTRUCTIONS

A construction is just like a mobile, except that it sits on a base and doesn't hang. It can have moving parts, or everything can be tied firmly in place. It can be made of one material like cardboard, or wire, or rods. Or, like the big one on the opposite page, it can be a combination of all kinds of different things.

Just a plain piece of wood sticking out of a base would be pretty boring to look at. But if there's another piece of wood tied to it, it becomes a little more interesting. Let a few objects dangle from the stick, paint on some color, tie or tack on a variety of different things, and it can become really exciting to look at. And that's what a construction is—a putting together of all sorts of different shapes and materials.

Look at the constructions on these pages. Notice how the shapes are chosen and combined to make a lively, varied design. And look at the empty spaces *between* the shapes. After all, they are a part of the design too.

There are no rules for making a construction. Actually there are no rules for any kind of art. In art, you are your own boss. What you like is what is right!

e.

How To Make A Construction

1. Get some cardboard, some thin wooden rods (dowels), or twigs, or wire. Get a piece of corrugated cardboard for a base. See if you can find some interesting-looking objects like colored paper, or leaves, or scraps of wood, or odds and ends of any kind. Try to find materials with different kinds of feeling or "texture," like bits of silk, sandpaper, steel wool, or bark. And you will probably need some string or thin wire.

2. Start by cutting out some cardboard shapes. Paint them. You may want to cut holes or spaces in them.

3. Try cutting little slots in the cardboard shapes and fitting one into another.

4. Poke the wire or twigs or dowels through the holes in the cardboard. Tie them in place where necessary.

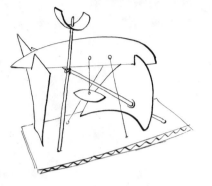

5. Now combine some of these things in as interesting and lively a design as possible. (You don't have to use everything.) See what shapes look well together, and what colors look well next to one another.

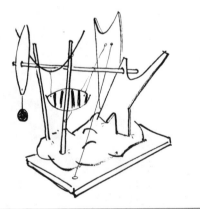

6. Try gluing on different things, or let some objects dangle from a string. If there is a stapler around, you can use that for fastening things together.

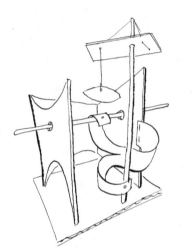

7. If you have trouble getting everything to stand up in place, use a lump of clay as a base and stick things into that.

8. Keep turning your construction as you work on it. See how it looks from all sides. Make sure it's not a jumble.

MASKS

These masks are a special kind of sculpture. They were made not as objects of art but as something to be used in tribal ceremonies or religious dances or dramatic performances.

They are supposed to look like powerful gods or protective spirits. That's why they rarely look like a real face. If the protective spirit was thought to look like some kind of animal, the mask was made to look like that animal, and the chief medicine man or witch doctor would wear it or dance in it while praying for special favors from that particular spirit. They are fierce and fanciful—sometimes even frightening.

Masks are often decorated with beads and feathers and usually painted in red, brown, black, and white.

A wooden mask is terribly heavy and uncomfortable to wear, but a papier-mâché mask is light and easy to wear or fun to hang up on a wall. It can be wild and ferocious, or funny, or sad. It can be like a clown, like an animal, like anything in the world—or like anything that *isn't* in the world! The more fantastic the better.

f.

b.

e.

d.

c.

g.

35

How To Make A Mask Out Of Papier-Mâché

1. To make a mask you'll need some clay, some newspapers, and some paper-hanger's paste. You can get the paste at any paint or hardware store. The mask will have to be started one day and finished off a few days later, because it has to dry for several days before it hardens and can be painted.

2. The first step is to make the shape of the mask roughly in clay. Let your imagination run free—the more fanciful the better.

3. Get some newspapers and rip them into long thin strips. About an inch wide is good.

4. Fill a small bowl half-full of water. Mix the paste into the water until the mixture begins to get thick and gooey.

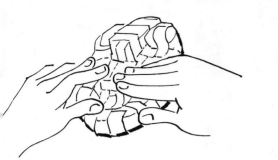

5. Then dip the strips into the paste, one at a time, and place them over the clay. Keep adding one strip over the other, criss-crossing them. Press each strip down and smooth it so that there are no air bubbles caught under the paper. If the paper gets too wet and mushy put on a dry strip now and then.

6. Keep adding more strips until you have twenty or thirty layers of paper over the clay. Shape the soggy paper with your fingers until you have the exact shapes that you want. Then put it aside and let it dry for several days. When it does dry, it will be hard and quite strong.

7. After the mask is dry, turn it upside down and take out the clay. Trim the edges of the paper with a heavy pair of scissors. Drill a hole in each side, so that you can attach a string. If you want to wear the mask, cut out the eyes.

8. Paint it. Then glue on feathers or beads or long shreds of paper, or whatever else you feel like.

9. You can make several bird and animal masks, hang or fasten one above the other, and you have a totem pole!

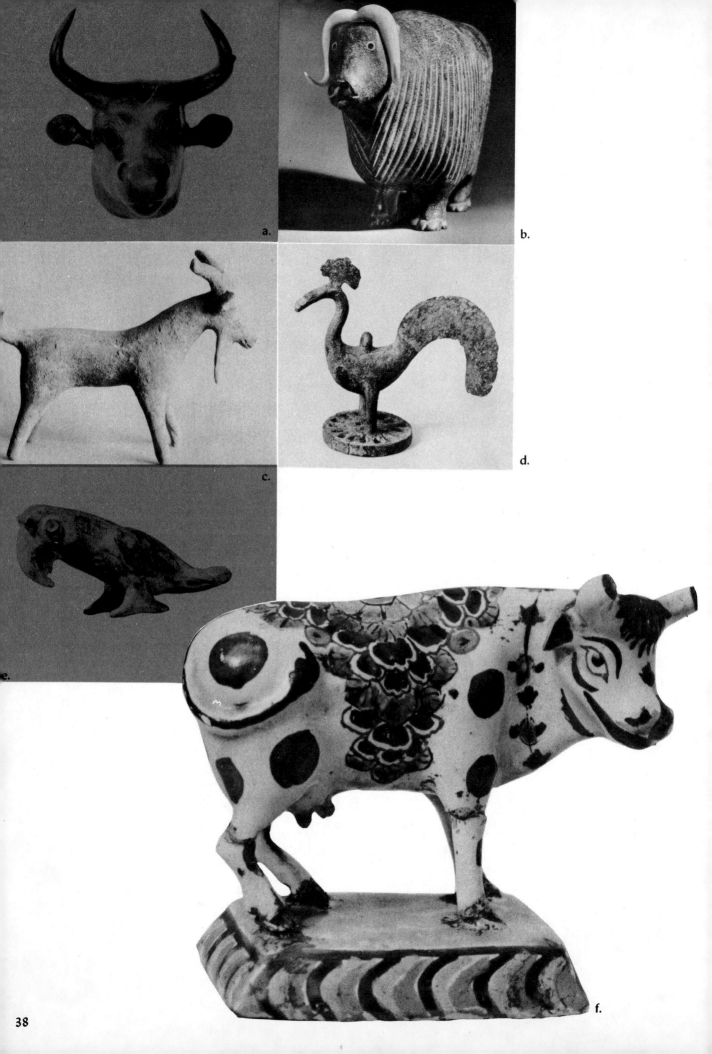

a.

b.

c.

d.

e.

f.

g.

ANIMALS

You'd have to look a long, long time before you'd find a real cow with a bunch of flowers painted on its side, but when it comes to a *sculpture*-cow anything can happen!

The sculptor who made that cow on the left just felt like painting flowers on its side, so he went ahead and did, and it looks just fine.

The sculptor who made the peacock liked the nice sweep of the tail, so he just concentrated on that and didn't even bother with the other things like feathers and wings and claws.

The artist who made the funny animal at the top of this page decided that stripes would look well on it, even though it isn't a tiger or a zebra. So he just went ahead and put them on.

This is one of the nicest things about any kind of art—you're free to do what you like. If you think something will look well, there's nothing in the world to keep you from trying it!

h.

i.

j.

How To Make A Plaster Cow

Plaster is a hard white material that is easy to paint, although it's tricky to handle. Lots of things look well in plaster—a cow, or a bull, or a polar bear—anything big and bulky. If you want to make a cow, for example, this is how you do it.

1. Get a big roll of thin, galvanized iron wire and a small bag of plaster of Paris. You can get them in any hardware store.

2. Start by making a simple skeleton or "armature" for the cow in the same way you made the horse out of pipe-cleaners earlier in the book.

3. Make sure the legs and neck aren't wobbly. Then wrap the wire around and around the armature, so that the shapes get a little stronger and bulkier. Wrap the wire on good and tight, and don't be afraid to use plenty of it. Wrap lots and lots of it on, until the cow begins to look fat. Try to get the lazy, saggy feeling of a cow.

4. When you're satisfied with the shape and pose of the cow, put it aside and mix your plaster. Follow these directions *exactly,* if you want the plaster to dry hard and strong. Get an old china cup. Fill it half full of water. *Slowly* sprinkle the plaster into the water without stirring, until the plaster fills up half the cup and absorbs all the water. Sixteen level teaspoons in half a cup of water is about right.

5. After you have the right amount of plaster in the water let it stand for half a minute. *Then* stir until the plaster is smooth and without lumps.

6. Now dip the cow, a part at a time, into the plaster. This will fill up all the little spaces between the wire.

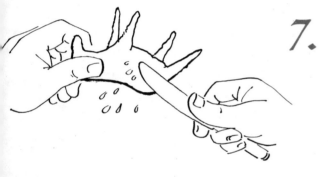

7. As the plaster begins to get thick and gooey, pick up some more with a dull knife and spread it on, building up the shapes you want. The plaster will get hard and unworkable in about four or five minutes, so you have to mix small batches and work fast.

8. When the plaster in the cup gets too hard to manage throw it out and mix another batch. Be sure the cup is cleaned thoroughly between each batch.

9. When you are finished, let the plaster dry for a day or two. Then, if you want, you can finish the surface with a file and sandpaper, or you can even whittle it with a knife. If you made the legs long and thin, you will have to work on them very carefully or they are apt to crack. Finally paint it. (Any kind of paint will do.)

Making A Bigger Plaster Cow

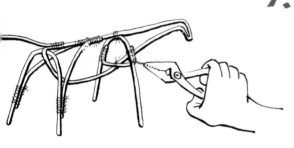

1. If you want to make a big cow, or some other big animal (and you may want to try making something good and big now), you'll have to make your armature a little differently because it will have to be stronger. Get some heavy, stiff wire and a pair of pliers. Build your armature out of this wire, using string or thin copper wire to tie the parts together. This is the most difficult part, so take your time and work slowly and carefully.

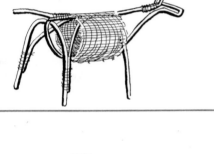

2. Cover the big, bulky places like the body with pieces of window screening. You can tie the pieces of screening in place with the thin wire.

3. Make this armature as neat and as strong as you can. Make sure everything is just the way you want it, because it is very hard to make changes once the plaster is hard. Cut up strips of burlap. Mix up some more plaster of Paris. Dip the strips of burlap into the plaster and wind them around the armature.

4. When the armature is completely covered with burlap, you can start to build up over it with the plaster. Then you can finish and paint it in the same way as you did the small cow.

Try making a figure in plaster—an acrobat hanging from a trapeze, or a boy and a girl on a see-saw, or a polar bear.

Wood Carving

If you've ever whittled a piece of wood with a penknife, or if you've even cut a piece of clay or plaster off of where it didn't belong, then you've carved. Carving is simply the process of removing material to get to the forms underneath. First you have to imagine the statue "imprisoned" inside the block of wood or stone, and then it's your job to release it!

Wood is easy to carve. You'll need a gouge, and a straight-edge chisel, and a mallet to hammer with. If the piece of wood you're working on isn't too hard (pine or oak are good) or too big, you can probably get by with a regular penknife.

Look at the grain of the wood and try to make it fit into your design. If you're making something large, put the wood in a vise so that it won't slide around as you work.

a.

b.

c.

d.

Stone Carving

The first sculptures ever made were done in the time of the cave man, and they were carved out of stone.

If you find a piece of stone that's not too hard, and if you feel like working slowly and carefully, you can carve it with steel chisels like the ones shown.

You'll have to make your design fit the stone, and you'll have to avoid sharp projections, which are difficult to carve and likely to break off. When you work, be sure to wear sun glasses or safety goggles to keep chips from flying into your eyes.

In both stone and wood, the simpler and more compact forms like fishes, or birds, or lumpy, fat figures are easiest to start with.

q.

Now you know the simple, basic ways of handling the materials of sculpture. You've seen the way the Indians and Egyptians and Etruscans and many others have used these materials to express their ideas and feelings.

But the things you've made, and the things you will go on to make are different, because sculpture, like any other art, is always an individual and a personal matter. The way you feel about something, what you see, what you make is yours and yours alone. If others see what you've done and like it—so much the better. But don't worry about pleasing other people. Please yourself first!

Don't be afraid to try out your own ideas. Don't hesitate to make your own discoveries. Now you're on your own.

OTHER BOOKS ON SCULPTURE

ZORACH EXPLAINS SCULPTURE, by William Zorach, American Artists Group.

SCULPTURE INSIDE AND OUT, by Malvina Hoffman, W. W. Norton and Co.

THE SCULPTOR'S WAY, by Brenda Putnam, Farrar and Rinehart.

SCULPTURE; PRINCIPLES AND PRACTICE, by Louis Slobodkin, World Publishing Company.

THE MATERIALS AND METHODS OF SCULPTURE, by Jack Rich, Oxford University Press.

ABOUT THE ILLUSTRATIONS

HORSES

a. HORSE, bronze, by Leonardo Da Vinci, Metropolitan Museum of Art. b. HORSE, bronze, by Edgar Degas, Metropolitan Museum of Art. c. MAN ON HORSE, terra cotta, Cypriote (1000-600 B.C.), Metropolitan Museum of Art. d. HORSE AND RIDER, bronze, by Marino Marini, Museum of Modern Art. e. HORSE AND RIDER, aquamanile, North European XIV Century, Metropolitan Museum of Art (Cloisters Collection). f. HORSE, bronze, archaic, American Museum of Natural History. g. HORSE, bronze, Greek VIII Century B.C., Metropolitan Museum of Art. h. HORSE, bronze, Greek V Century B.C., Metropolitan Museum of Art. i. HAUT ECOLE, bronze, by Amory C. Simons, Metropolitan Museum of Art.

LIONS

a. HEAD OF A LION (detail from a chimaera), bronze, Etruscan, Archaeological Museum, Florence, Italy. b. SEATED LION, stone, Chinese (Tang Period), Metropolitan Museum of Art. c. LION, terra cotta, by the author. d. LION, limestone, Egyptian, Metropolitan Museum of Art. e. LION SEATED, bronze, Greek VI Century B.C. f. HEAD OF A LION, marble, Greek V Century B.C.

HEADS

a. HEAD, bronze, Nigeria, Africa, American Museum of Natural History. b. FIGURINE (detail), terra cotta, probably Vera Cruz, Mexico, American Museum of Natural History. c. HEAD, terra cotta, Cypriote, Metropolitan Museum of Art. d. SEATED BISHOP (detail), polychromed wood, Flemish XIII Century, Cleveland Museum of Art, gift of John D. Rockefeller, Jr. e. HEAD, marble, Roman copy of a Greek head, Metropolitan Museum of Art. f. FIGURE (detail), terra cotta, Queretaro, Mexico, American Museum of Natural History. g. QUEEN HAT-SHEP-SUT, granite, Egypt XVIII Dynasty, about 1485 B.C., Metropolitan Museum of Art. h. CARVED STONE, Queriquerins Island, Bay of Conception, Chile, American Museum of Natural History. i. HEAD, stone, Easter Islands, American Museum of Natural History. j. HEAD OF BUDDHA, bronze, Indian, author's collection. k. HEAD, terra cotta, Cypriote VII Century B.C., Metropolitan Museum of Art. l. MADONNA AND CHILD (detail), oak, Eastern French or Flemish, Cleveland Museum of Art, gift of John D. Rockefeller, Jr.

FIGURES

a. MAN WITH A HARP, marble, Cycladic 2500 B.C., Metropolitan Museum of Art. b. THE RUNNERS, bronze, by Gerhard Marcks, Museum of Modern Art, gift of Mrs. John D. Rockefeller, Jr. c. SEATED FIGURE, terra cotta, archaic culture, Mexico, American Museum of Natural History. d. ESKIMO CARVING, stone, by an unknown Eskimo artist from Port Harrison, Department of Northern Affairs and Natural Resources, Canada. e. f. g. h. i. j. DANCERS, bronze, by Edgar Degas, Metropolitan Museum of Art. k. NAVIGATOR, wood, Old Dartmouth Historical and Whaling Museum. l. WARRIOR, bronze, Etruscan, Metropolitan Museum of Art. m. WARRIOR WITH SPEAR, terra cotta, Tarascan, Mexico, Museum of Art of the Rhode Island School of Design. n. FIGURE, Tepic, Mexico, American Museum of Natural History. o. ACROBATS, plaster, by the author. p. RECLINING FIGURE, cast stone, by Henry Moore, Washington University Art Collection. q. (page 46) "WELL, SO LONG NOW," plaster, by the author, collection of the publisher.

MOBILES

a. BLACK SPREAD, metal and wire, by Alexander Calder, Des Moines Art Center, Edmundson Collection. b. GAD-ABOUT, wire, cardboard, pebbles, brush, and typewriter erasers, by the author.

CONSTRUCTIONS

a. SPINY, aluminum, by Alexander Calder, Private Collection, New York. b. KOUROS, marble, by Isamu Noguchi, Metropolitan Museum of Art. c. NUTCRACKER-DUSTER, sheet-metal, feather, corks, wrench, wire, brush, by the author. d. THE PALACE AT 4 A.M., wood, glass, wire, string, by Alberto Giacometti, Museum of Modern Art. e. CITY LANDSCAPE, bronze, by the author.

MASKS

a. FACE PLATE FROM GABLE OF MEN'S HOUSE, wood, New Guinea, American Museum of Natural History. b. WOODEN MASK, Bampende Colony, Africa, American Museum of Natural History. c. DRAMATIC MASK, wood, Java, American Museum of Natural History. d. DANCING MASK, wood and dyed sage bark, New Guinea, American Museum of Natural History. e. MASK, wood and feathers, Alaska, American Museum of Natural History. f. ELEPHANT MASK, wood, Bampende Colony, Africa, American Museum of Natural History. g. DRAMATIC MASK, wood, Java, American Museum of Natural History.

ANIMALS

a. HEAD OF BULL, bronze, archaic Greek, American Museum of Natural History. b. MUSK-OX, stone, by Akeeaktashuk, Ellesmere Island, Canada, Collection of Mr. Bert Beaver. c. GOAT, terra cotta, archaic Greek, Metropolitan Museum of Art. d. PEACOCK, bronze, Greek VIII Century B.C., Metropolitan Museum of Art. e. PARROT, terra cotta, Colima style, Mexico, American Museum of Natural History. f. COW, Delft, Dutch 18th Century, Metropolitan Museum of Art. g. OX, terra cotta, Greek (about 1400-1100 B.C.), Metropolitan Museum of Art. h. FALCON, bronze, European (XII-XIII Century), Metropolitan Museum of Art, Cloisters Collection. i. STANDING BULL, bronze, by Elie Nadelman, Museum of Modern Art, gift of Mrs. Elie Nadelman. j. POLAR BEAR, stone, by Tikeetuk, Baffin Island, Canada, Collection of Mr. Bert Beaver.

CARVING

a. DANCER, wood, by Glen Chamberlain, Sculpture Center Gallery. b. FETISH FIGURE, wood, Africa, American Museum of Natural History. c. TRIUMPH OF THE EGG, I, granite, by John B. Flannagan, Museum of Modern Art. d. HEAD OF CHRIST, granite, by William Zorach, The Museum of Modern Art.